BEAUTIFUL CALIFORNIA

A Sunset Pictorial

BEAUTIFUL CALIFORNIA

Lane Publishing Co., Menlo Park, California

ED COOPER

Edited by Elizabeth Hogan

Design: Richard Lemen

Front Cover: California poppies, the state flower, carpet a northern California hillside; photograph by Betty Randall. Back Cover: Yosemite Valley in a winter mood; photograph by Tom Tracy. Title Page: Rolling hills around Walnut Creek, east of San Francisco; photograph by Ted Streshinsky. Map by Dick Cole.

Special thanks go to Barbara J. Braasch, Barbara Gibson, and Will Kirkman for their valuable assistance in gathering, organizing, and checking information.

Editor, Sunset Books: David E. Clark

Fifth Printing May 1979

This book was printed and bound by Kingsport Press, Kingsport, Tennessee, from litho film prepared by Graphic Arts Center, Portland, Oregon. Body type is Aster, type for heads is Bookman Meola, composed by Paul O. Geisey/Adcrafters, Portland. Paper for pages is Velvo Enamel made by Westvaco Corp., Luke, Maryland.

Contents

Beautiful California 6

The North Coast 10

Wine Country. 22

San Francisco & the Bay Area 34

The Central Coast 70

The Los Angeles Area. 90

San Diego. 128

California's Desert 148

The Sierra Nevada 168

Gold Rush Country. 190

The Central Valley 202

The Northern Mountains. 212

Index 224

Beautiful California

Ocean surf and mountain meadows, farms, vineyards, and desert sand . . . it's the diversity, the grandeur, and the contrasts of California's scenic attractions that make the Golden State so appealing.

One of the prizes of California is the Pacific shore, 1,100 miles long. In the north you see wind-carved bluffs rising into dense forests nurtured by winter rains and summer fog. The southern coast—with miles of sandy beaches, warmer water, and sunny days—offers swimming, surfing, or relaxing on a beach towel.

Ranging along much of the coast is a series of mountains, the Coast Range, green with redwoods and Douglas fir or golden where oaks and grasses mingle. Jutting down from Oregon and Washington into northern California are the volcanic Cascades. But California's mountain paradise lies in the Sierra Nevada, one single mountain upthrust running 400 miles along the eastern side of the state. In the Sierra are unparalleled gems, such as Lake Tahoe, Tuolumne Meadows, Palisades Glacier, Yosemite Falls, the giant sequoias, and Mt. Whitney.

Sandwiched between the Coast and Sierra ranges, the farms of the Central Valley extend for 465 miles through the center of the state. Here is California's heartland, where the right combination of rich soil, enough water, and a moderate climate parlay over 200 crops into multi-billion dollar harvests.

An intriguing and bizarre landscape covers California's southeastern section, with the Mojave and Colorado deserts stretching over one-fifth of the state. Robbed of any moisture by intervening mountains, the desert consists of barren mountains and valleys, vegetation that has learned to adapt to a harsh climate, washes created by flash floods, vast expanses of sand dunes, salt plains, and vibrant colors created by the moods of the sky.

Although much of California's visual appeal lies in its natural landscape, some of its famous sights are a combination of man and nature, such as the Golden Gate Bridge, Pebble Beach Golf Course, Hearst Castle, Santa Barbara nestled between mountains and sea, Newport Beach's elegant waterfront, and San Diego's skyline as viewed from Pt. Loma.

Buildings and mementoes of California's colorful past add a nostalgic note to the landscape. California belonged to Spain for two centuries before the Spanish began to colonize it in the 1770s. In the next 80 years, they established a chain of missions and built presidios for their soldiers and haciendas for the land-grant ranchers which influenced later architectural styles in California. Many of the struc-

High Sierra meadow

Death Valley National Monument

Sacramento Valley

Coast redwoods

Newport Beach

Redwood
National Park

THE NORTHERN
MOUNTAINS

Lassen Volcanic
National Park

THE NORTH COAST

WINE
COUNTRY

THE SIERRA NEVADA

GOLD RUSH COUNTRY

THE CENTRAL VALLEY

Pt. Reyes
National
Seashore

Muir Woods
National Monument

Yosemite National Park

SAN FRANCISCO
AND THE BAY AREA

Devils Postpile
National
Monument

Kings Canyon and
Sequoia National Parks

THE CENTRAL COAST

THE
LOS ANGELES
AREA

Within California's boundaries
*lie the scenic wonders of
an entire continent—seashore,
valleys, mountains, and deserts.
To give the best overall view of
each, we've broken these geo-
graphical areas down further,
devoting a chapter to the North
Coast, the Central Coast, Wine Country, the Northern Mountains, the
Central Valley, Gold Rush Country, the
Sierra Nevada, and the Desert. In addition,
we've included chapters on California's
three largest and very unique metropolitan
areas—San Francisco, Los Angeles, and
San Diego.*

tures managed to survive the ravages of time and have been restored to their original form.

Nations other than Spain had their sights set on California. In 1812 Russia established a colony of fur traders 100 miles north of San Francisco. When Mexico revolted against Spain in 1822, California joined the rebel cause and became a province of the Empire of Mexico–a status it maintained until the territory was ceded to the United States by the Treaty of 1848, ending the Mexican-American War. Two years later Congress admitted California to the Union.

In that two-year interval, the character of California was changed forever, for in 1848, James Marshall found traces of gold in the American River–a discovery that touched off a mad race West to strike it rich in the Sierra foothills. Relics of the Gold Rush era exist today; some have been restored or refurbished while others stand in abandoned decay.

The Gold Rush launched California on a course of spiraling growth that has continued ever since. San Francisco and Sacramento grew with the Gold Rush. With the completion of the transcontinental railroad in 1869 and its extension to southern California a few years later, thousands of settlers flocked to "the perfect paradise, the land of perpetual spring." Industry followed, and more people came to live in the bountiful state.

Today California is the most populous state in the Union, with a majority of the population concentrated in the San Francisco Bay Area, the Los Angeles area, and San Diego County. A coastal location plus a benevolent climate have made these metropolitan areas the three largest in the state.

The large number of people California has attracted has had its effect on the land. Concrete freeways criss-cross cities and connect all corners of the state. Smog and haze are no longer unique to Los Angeles; San Francisco Bay Area pollution blows to outlying communities, while Los Angeles smog appears 300 miles northeast in Death Valley National Monument. Scenic hillsides support subdivisions, pushing city limits further out into the countryside. Restrictions on visitor use had to be imposed at Yosemite National Park because it was being "loved to death."

Fortunately, a majority of the state's natural splendors stand protected within national parks, monuments, and forests and state parks. Today's planners seem to be cognizant of the problems of dealing with the future as well as preserving the past. Freeways are being designed to blend in with the landscape. A master plan for the entire coast was drawn up in the mid-1970s. Some forest and park areas have been given wilderness status to preserve the solitude of the back country. Hopefully, as the population of California continues to grow, its residents will continue to be aware of the importance of saving the best of their state for future generations.

Death Valley National Monument

CALIFORNIA'S DESERT

Joshua Tree National Monument

SAN DIEGO

The North Coast

Rocky cliffs, crashing surf, towering redwoods, perennial fog, and picturesque villages sum up the North Coast's attractions.

Unlike the southern California coast, which caters to swimmers, sailers, surfers, and sun worshipers, the North Coast welcomes ocean "browsers," those who like to walk the beaches or the wave-battered bluffs. All along the North Coast, the air is crisp and clear—except for thick morning and evening summertime fog.

Cathedral-like groves of the coast redwood (Sequoia sempervirens) thrive on the misty, damp, cool air of the North Coast. Native to the area, they are protected in Redwood National Park and in a string of state parks that stretch from the Oregon border south to Monterey County.

Eureka, in the far north, is the North Coast's largest city, but the Mendocino area—with its quaint New England charm, nostalgic inns and hotels, leisurely pace, and fishing village—draws vacationers. Other popular destinations are Pt. Reyes National Seashore and the numerous state beaches that line the entire North Coast.

Native Home
of the Coast Redwood

HARALD SUND

BETTY RANDALL

BETTY RANDALL

ROY MURPHY

Dense groves *of the majestic coast redwoods* (Sequoia sempervirens) *thrive along the foggy California coast from Redwood National Park south to Monterey County. Often growing higher than 300 feet, these giants of nature are the world's tallest trees. In their moist shade sprout a rich variety of ferns, wildflowers (skunk cabbage shown above), and shrubs. Protected in Prairie Creek Redwoods State Park are four herds (about 200 total) of Roosevelt elk, actually not elk at all but king-size members of the deer family.*

Summer fog, *common along the Northern California coast, steals across Crescent City's rock-studded beach and muffles the voice of the retreating tide. Here the encroaching gray mist begins to envelop solitary Battery Point lighthouse. You walk two hundred yards across a reef to reach the nautical museum—but only at low tide.*

Foggy Days along California's Coast

BETTY RANDALL

Rhododendrons and redwoods *flourish on frequent visits of drifting fog. Salty sea breezes drive chill mists into thick forests that stretch along the North Coast for some 350 miles.*

Victorian Touches along the North Coast

"The more the better" *must have been lumber baron William Carson's thinking when he had his mansion in Eureka (left) adorned with gables, balconies, and carved moldings. Built in 1885, the Carson home remained in the family for three generations; in 1950 a local organization took it over. A more delicate example of the Victorian era is Mendocino's MacCallum House (above), restored and opened as an inn in 1975.*

RUSSELL LAMB

ED COOPER

Gingerbread Mansion *in Ferndale takes its name from the facade rich in fancy lathe work. The ornate house, built in 1898, belonged to Dr. Hogan J. Ring, then served as the town hospital. Now it holds several apartments.*

First a remote mill town, *now an art colony, picturesque*
Mendocino remains a museum of carpenter's
Gothic houses and transplanted New England charm.
The town grew up—with a plethora of saloons, hotels,
and a Chinatown—around a lumber mill in the 1850s.

Mast confusion *reigns where trawlers and trollers gather at the docks in Noyo's harbor. Until stormy weather ends the season in October, commercial and sport fishermen make Noyo a base for fishing North Coast waters.*

Fishing– for Business or for Fun

Elbow to elbow, *salmon and steel-head anglers seek their fortune at the mouth of the Klamath River as fish come in to spawn. At Humboldt Bay (below), clammers stab the sand at low tide.*

Dip-netters *strain ocean breakers for smelt during the summer runs along the coast—all the way from the Alaskan gulf to Point Conception.*

Pt. Reyes...
A Wilderness
Seashore

The many moods *of Pt. Reyes National Seashore attract beachcomber, birdwatcher, rockhound, and hiker. Through a system of trails, the visitor can explore the different aspects of the peninsula, from the lush valley along Meadow Trail (left) to the rugged seashore.*

PHOTOS: JACK McDOWELL

Uniform breakers curl *onto Drake's Beach (left), one of the few on the peninsula calm enough for swimming. Rocky outcroppings (above) at Drake's Bay—believed to be the spot where Sir Francis Drake beached his vessel, the Golden Hinde, in 1579—protect the strand from blustering northwest winds.*

Wine Country

The Napa and Sonoma valleys, lying northeast of San Francisco, are names synonymous with California wine. Long straight rows of vines blanket much of Napa's valley floor, and curving rows bend around steep hillsides. In Sonoma, vineyards circle a former pueblo and stretch north of town through narrowing hills. In the midst of all this grape growing lie some 50 wineries (10 in Sonoma and 40 in Napa), many bearing old established names in wine.

Wine making came first to Sonoma. In the 1830s grapes were growing at the Sonoma mission. Mexican General Vallejo took over the vineyards and, for a while, ran a lively competition with Agoston Haraszthy, founder of Buena Vista winery and the father of California wine making. Over in Napa, George Yount planted a vineyard in the 1840s for personal use; the first commercial wine in this valley was made in 1861 by German emigrant Charles Krug.

Today visitors flock to the wine country to tour the cellars, to sample the wines, and to enjoy the scenic and tranquil countryside. Although most people visit the valleys in the summer, fall is the liveliest time of year –when the grape harvest is on.

Napa and Sonoma—Valleys of Vineyards

Heart of California's wine country *lies in the Napa and Sonoma valleys, where about 40,000 acres of vines stretch over valley floors, up and over hillsides, and around winery buildings. With the right combination of care and luck, grapes from the vineyards yield roughly 16 million gallons of red and white table wines each year.*

PHOTOS: TED STRESHINSKY

Christian Brothers winery *near Napa stands above vineyards where harvesters gather ripe grapes. The massive structure of hand-cut native sandstone dates back to 1903.*

Hanzell winery, *in the Sonoma Valley, copies the architecture of the Clos de Vougeot in Burgundy. Wines produced at Hanzell age in barrels made of oak from the French forests of the Limousin.*

Sterling Winery, *starch white and modern with Mediterranean look, sits on a knoll overlooking the Napa Valley. Stained-glass windows, carved doors, and bells suggest a monastic mood.*

The Look of Wineries: Traditional to Contemporary

Chateau Chevalier's *romantic stone building perches on a steep slope in the Napa Valley north of St. Helena. Terraced vineyards surround this lovely cellar, built in 1891.*

Souverain of Alexander Valley *is a relative newcomer (1974) to the wine country scene. Drawn with clean, spare lines and twin towers, this winery imitates old hop barns scattered across the northern Sonoma County countryside.*

PHOTOS: TED STRESHINSKY

Wine Touring and Tasting

Touring and tasting *have become celebrated pastimes among increasing numbers of wine fanciers, and winemakers of both large and small cellars welcome guests. Robert Mondavi Winery in Oakville offers either guided or informal tours through its ultramodern establishment.*

Picnic grounds *at Sonoma Vineyards convert into an open-air concert hall for a summer season of symphonies and jazz and rock concerts. Inside the winery, up the triangular stair-case, elevated balconies overlook wine production.*

Tasting room *at Sterling Vineyards is elegant, airy, and a pleasant end to a self-guided tour. Chenin Blanc, Chardonnay, Cabernet Sauvignon, Pinot Noir, and Zinfandel typify varietals available for sampling.*

From Vines to Wine

A long, taut season *stretches from infant berries to mature fruit. Like anxious parents, vineyardists watch over their vines until the last threat of frost or pest has vanished. Come September and October, the heady aroma of ripened grapes fills the air, and the harvest is on.*

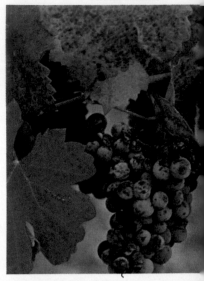

After the fall harvest, *the vintner's gamble moves indoors, where the metamorphosis from juice to wine occurs. Following fermentation, new wines mature (some in fine old oak casks) until the time comes to bottle, label, and market the vintage.*

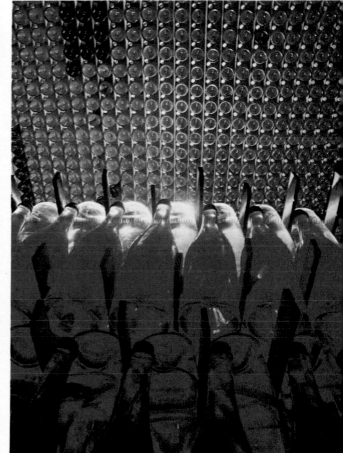

In Addition to Wine...

California's colorful past *resurfaces in Sonoma. You can see Mission San Francisco Solano and "Lachryma Montis," Mexican General Mariano Vallejo's home (below). The historic Bear Flag Revolt of 1846 began here.*

PHOTOS: TED STRESHINSKY

Wolf House, *a dream-turned-nightmare, stands in stony ruin at Jack London State Historic Park. Fire destroyed the enormous house in 1913, only days before the popular writer and his wife, Charmian, were to move in.*

Tranquil central plaza *of Sonoma offers its grassy shade to a group of school children. General Vallejo himself surveyed this site in 1834. In his time the plaza held dog and raccoon fights, wild horse rides, races, fiestas, and parades.*

San Francisco
& the Bay Area

Few cities in the world have the unique character of San Francisco. What makes it so special?

Referred to simply as "the city" by Northern Californians, San Francisco sits on the hilly tip of a peninsula. The ocean on the west and a bay on the north and east keep San Francisco pleasantly warm in winter and naturally air-conditioned in summer. The geography of the city—water on three sides—didn't impede its growth. Instead of growing out, San Francisco just grew close together and high.

San Francisco, built on some 40 hills, is a city of views. Twin Peaks offers the most encompassing view of the entire city. From Nob and Russian hills, you look down past layered buildings to the bay below.

Since the late 1800s, cable cars and curbside flower stands have been part of the San Francisco scene. Mansions built by railroad barons and bonanza kings are now hotels; abandoned factories and warehouses have been transformed into architectural attractions; and Victorian houses— true San Francisco classics—continue to be reclaimed and restored to their original elegance.

Since the Gold Rush turned the dozing Spanish village of Yerba Buena into a boom town, international neighborhoods have been contributing heavily to the city's cultural and culinary diversity. In San Francisco is one of the largest Oriental communities in the western world.

Beyond the boundaries of the city lie numerous communities that make up the San Francisco Bay Area. Across the Golden Gate Bridge to the north is Marin County; across the Bay Bridge spread the East Bay communities, including Berkeley and Oakland; and stretching 40 miles to the south is the Peninsula, culminating in the urban sprawl of San Jose.

THE SAN FRANCISCO BAY AREA

The Golden Gate Bridge—*built where it was said a bridge couldn't be built—has become a San Francisco symbol. The single, 4200-foot span is one of the most spectacular engineering feats of all time.*

San Francisco– Everybody's Favorite Landmarks

Cable cars, *a means of transportation around San Francisco since 1873, continue to delight natives and visitors who flood the moving national landmarks for thrilling rides across the most congested part of town.*

TOM TRACY

Colorful flower stands *display seasons by streetside, rain or shine. Since the 1880s, curbside florists have filled their tubs with locally-grown flowers, supplying shoppers with cut flowers the year around.*

PETER FRONK

Downtown San Francisco... Shopping, Strolling, Sightseeing

A whimsical history of San Francisco winds around the circular Children's Fountain at the Hyatt hotel plaza near Union Square. The step-climbing bas-relief was created by sculptress Ruth Asawa.

PHOTOS: TED STRESHINSKY

Fashionable department stores and specialty shops surrounding Union Square invite spender and browser alike. This merchandise mecca attracts shoppers from all over the West.

Relaxing *on Union Square's grassy, manicured slope is a popular midday pastime for San Franciscans. Across Powell Street is elegant St. Francis Hotel.*

THE SAN FRANCISCO BAY AREA **39**

Leafy enclave *of MacArthur Park*
suggests the great outdoors inside a renovated paper warehouse. Skylight wells, aviary, and waterfall keep the setting open and airy.

Waterfront renewal project *transformed San Francisco's colorful but blighted produce market district into the Golden Gateway, a 51-acre area between Battery Street and the Embarcadero. This modern complex contains commercial buildings, apartment towers, town houses, shops, fountains, and parks.*

Golden Gateway: A Renaissance along the Bay

Sight and sound of water *are among the attractions of the Golden Gateway. The Woodward fountain (below) sprouts, like a bunch of dandelions, out of a cobblestone base at Maritime Plaza. Stepping stones through Vaillancourt Fountain (right) in the Justin Herman Plaza take visitors on a misty, dripping, splashing tour.*

PHOTOS: PETER FRONK

The North Waterfront: Fisherman's Wharf to Fort Point

At Fisherman's Wharf *(above), sidewalk stalls and steaming cauldrons loaded with fresh crab and shrimp attract seafood lovers. Mazes of nearby shops, restaurants, and galleries have transformed a defunct cannery (right) and an old chocolate factory into beguiling waterfront attractions.*

Golden Gate Promenade, *3½ miles of shoreline between Fort Point and Aquatic Park, welcomes walkers. This addition to the Golden Gate National Recreation Area offers first-rate views of the city skyline to the east and the Golden Gate Bridge to the west.*

Fort Point, *a pre-Civil War military bastion, was built in 1861 to guard the Golden Gate. Now a national historic site, the forbidding-looking fortress stands half-hidden under the south tower of the Golden Gate Bridge.*

TED STRESHINSKY

THE SAN FRANCISCO BAY AREA **43**

Eastern orthodoxy *is preserved in the fabric of the Russian Holy Virgin Cathedral of the Church of Exile, on Geary Street. The onion domes and the icons along the facade have architectural roots in the Byzantine Empire.*

PHOTOS: TED STRESHINSKY

International San Francisco

Grant Avenue, *glittering Oriental transplant, runs through the commercial core of China-town, one of the largest Chinese communities in the Western world. Shops sell all sorts of gewgaws—and fine porcelain, ivory, and jade.*

"Little Italy," *at home in North Beach since the 1850s, contributes Italian delicatessens and restaurants, long loaves of sweet or sour bread, and a lively spirit to the ethnic variety of San Francisco.*

THE SAN FRANCISCO BAY AREA **45**

From the brow of Nob Hill, *steep California Street reflects San Francisco's paradoxical penchant for progress and love for the past. An occidental high-rise dwarfs a scarlet pagoda, and a cable car inches up the grade toward a hilltop view of the Bay Bridge.*

Hills, Hills, and more Hills

It takes patience *to climb the endless steps that scale Telegraph Hill on Kearny Street. "If you ever get tired of walking around the city," they say, "you can always lean against it."*

TED STRESHINSKY

JACK McDOWELL

Lombard Street *changes direction ten times as it winds back and forth around manicured hedges and blossoming hydrangeas in the space of one brick-paved block. The "Crookedest Street in the World" is on Russian Hill, between Hyde and Leavenworth.*

Golden Gate Park...
A Sunday Oasis
for City Dwellers

Music lovers *enjoy free concerts every Sunday afternoon (weather permitting) at the sheltered amphitheatre of the Music Concourse. Programs range from traditional marches, folk tunes, and blues, to rock or Bach.*

GLENN CHRISTIANSEN

Victorian flower conservatory *preserves multitudes of exotic plants and bright seasonal blooms within its glass shell. The delicate building, a replica of the Royal Conservatory at Kew Gardens, England, came disassembled from New York to San Francisco in 1878.*

In the peaceful *Japanese Tea Garden, a five-tiered pagoda overlooks meticulous gardens blooming with fragile cherry blossoms and azaleas in spring. Narrow paths meander by quiet pools and streams.*

GLENN CHRISTIANSEN

Manmade Stow Lake *and cultivated woods nearby hardly resemble the same land described in the 1860s as a "dreary waste of shifting sand hills where a blade of grass cannot be raised without four posts to support it."*

THE SAN FRANCISCO BAY AREA **49**

In a placid lagoon setting, *the Palace of Fine Arts survives as the only relic of the 1915 Panama-Pacific Exposition that celebrated Beauty, Progress, and the new Panama Canal. Designed by architect Bernard Maybeck and built to last only one year, the Palace was saved from ruin through a magnificent, impractical, civic campaign in the late 1950s.*

San Francisco's Grand Architecture

Refurbished row houses *(above) bring Victorian charm out of the past into Pacific Heights and the Western Addition, where the old-timers prevail. Atop Nob Hill (left), the stately mansion built by Comstock king James Flood is the only building on the hill to survive the 1906 earthquake and fire. Beyond it stands very Gothic Grace Cathedral.*

A Bold Look for a Traditional City

Beyond the stalwart charm *of Front Street (above), dramatic, exposed diagonal grids frame the Alcoa Building at Maritime Plaza. Transamerica's pyramidal "skysaver" (right) has the highest reach (853 feet) on San Francisco's skyline.*

Free-form, *walk-through sculpture at Embarcadero Plaza stands in sharp contrast against the Ferry Building, a vivid reminder of the days when ferry boats carried the traffic across San Francisco Bay. Canadian Armand Vaillancourt designed the controversial fountain, composed of 101 concrete boxes.*

PHOTOS: JACK McDOWELL

Likened to a majestic schooner *in full sail, new St. Mary's on Cathedral Hill is hailed as an architectural prodigy. Startling white marble contours and radiant slices of stained glass windows rise 190 feet above spacious brick plazas.*

Classic Views of a Classic Skyline

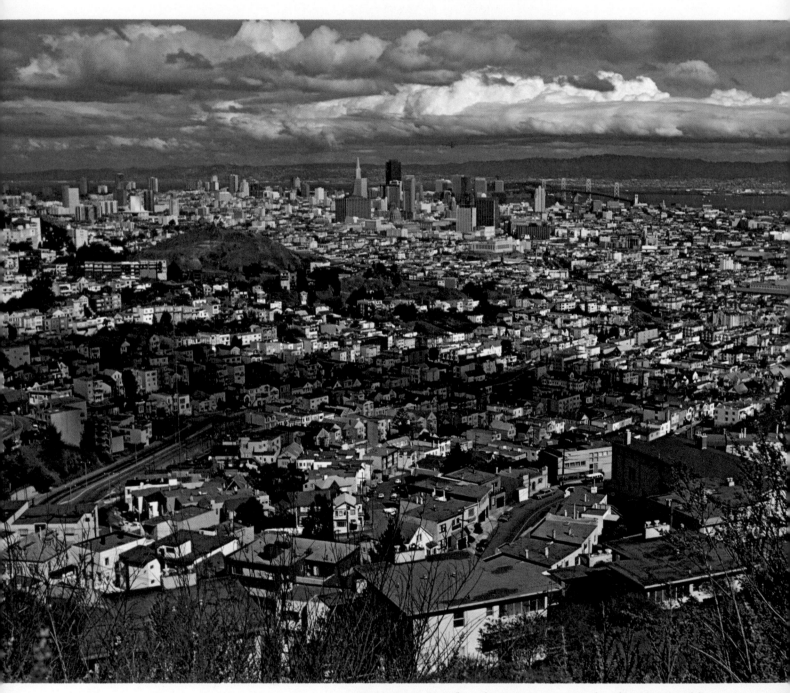

From Twin Peaks, *the San Francisco landscape sparkles under a dramatic sky. In the foreground tightly packed houses crowd the hillside, and in the distance sky-scraping highrises run almost to the watery edge of San Francisco Bay. Beyond the bay stretch the East Bay communities of Berkeley and Oakland.*

From Marin County (*top of page*) *or the East Bay, San Francisco's skyline dominates the horizon. Modern additions to "the City" (Transamerica Pyramid, Bank of America) dwarf old favorites (Coit Tower, Fairmont Hotel).*

North Bay's Natural Attractions

The rugged, open lands *of the Marin coast are practically all protected in state and national parks. At Marin Headlands, just north of the Golden Gate, the coastline plummets from bare-crested hills into deep waters. One exception is a pocket beach a few hundred yards west of the bridge.*

PHOTOS: JERRY FREDRICK

Virgin coast redwoods *grow in a cool canyon at the foot of Mount Tamalpais in 502-acre Muir Woods National Monument. At Audubon Canyon Ranch (right), common egrets rendezvous at a favorite nesting site for springtime rites of courtship.*

Wind-surfers *skate over the bay with a little help from a sail and a stiff breeze. The popular fledgling sport —like sailing and surfing— demands fast thinking and some fancy footwork.*

Marine Influence on Marin

Rolling through the Golden Gate, *a bank of fog begins to reach into Marin County's serene waterside communities. Belvedere Island, Tiburon (left foreground), and Sausalito (across Richardson Bay) are home ports for yachtsmen and fishermen.*

Rustic houses *cling to steep hillsides above Sausalito where shops and open-deck restaurants hug the waterfront. On weekends Richardson Bay becomes a playground for sailing vessels of every rank.*

TOM TRACY

East Bay: Emphasis on Education

Mills College, *liberal arts college for women, occupies a parklike setting in east Oakland. Its oldest building, Victorian-style Mills Hall, went up in 1871 when the school moved from Benicia.*

Boldly-designed *Lawrence Hall of Science above the Berkeley campus is a research and teaching facility, but the complex admits visitors to exhibits and laboratories demonstrating scientific principles.*

In Berkeley, *the University of California's landmark Campanile (a copy of the bell tower in Venice) rises 307 feet above tree-shaded lawns and buildings at this oldest of all the state's nine university campuses.*

Part gallery, part garden, *the Oakland Museum is as famous for its architecture as it is for its exhibits on California history, art, and natural science.*

Oakland's Highlights

Lake Merritt's *salty blue waters form the only tidal lake in the heart of an American city. Lakeside attractions include botanical gardens, a wild duck refuge, a science center, and a children's storybook park. Surrounding the 155-acre body of water are a shoreline drive and office and apartment buildings.*

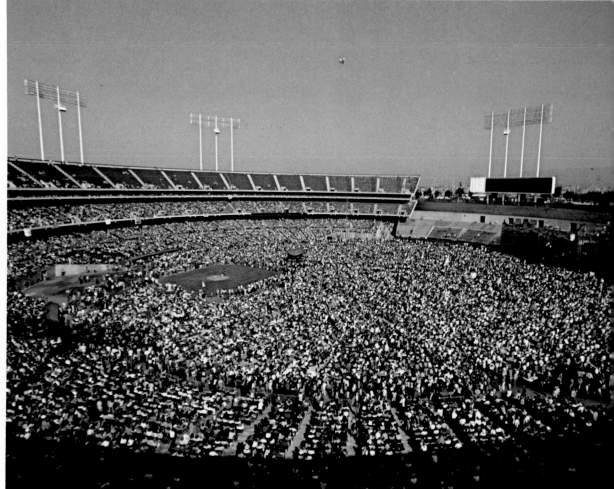

An "Afternoon on the Green" *draws thousands to open-air concerts at the Oakland Coliseum. In addition, the circular stadium hosts professional football and baseball games. In the adjoining circular indoor arena, basketball games, ice and stage shows, circuses, and civic and cultural events take place.*

Bart-Connecting Link between East Bay Cities and "the City"

Gliding over its track *with high-speed ease, a BART train whisks East Bay passengers from the Walnut Creek area to work in San Francisco. The Bay Area Rapid Transit System is one of the most ambitious public transport projects in U.S. history and is California's only mass transit system. Operating above and underground, it links nine San Francisco stations with 25 points in the East Bay.*

TED STRESHINSKY

Peninsula Showplaces

Stanford University, *founded in 1883 by railroad baron Leland Stanford and his wife in memory of their son, occupies 8,200 acres. Memorial Church, with its exquisite Venetian mosaics and stained glass windows, lies at the heart of the campus—a 17-acre quadrangle of native sandstone buildings.*

Allied Arts Guild *in Menlo Park occupies a 3½-acre site that was originally part of the vast Spanish land grant El Rancho de las Pulgas. It features colorful gardens and Spanish-style buildings housing small specialty shops.*

Sunset Magazine and Sunset Books *welcome guests to their editorial and business offices in Menlo Park. Here are testing kitchens and showplace gardens for plants that grow in all sections of the Pacific Coast.*

Surfing's fair, *swimming's good, and the fishing's fine at Santa Cruz, a summer destination for Bay Area residents. Beyond the long municipal pier, the old boardwalk sports a razz-matazz of carnival rides, hot dog stands, and games at the Penny Arcade.*

Jazz, folk, and classical *musicians play for the pleasure of guests at Paul Masson's Mountain Winery in the hills above Saratoga. Open-air concerts with champagne intermissions have been a weekend cellar tradition since 1958.*

JERRY FREDRICK

Potpourri of Activities South of the Bay

"Turn of the Century" *provides a thrilling—but scary—45 mph roller coaster ride at Marriott's Great America in Santa Clara. The family fun park, with an American history theme, features wild rides, shows, and shops.*

PHOTOS: JERRY FREDRICK

TOM TRACY

Stairs that lead nowhere, *doors to brick walls, and 10,000 windows make Sarah Winchester's 160-room Mystery House in San Jose most bizarre. Heiress to the rifle fortune, Mrs. Winchester believed she would continue to live as long as she continued to build.*

The Central Coast

The Central Coast, from Monterey south to Santa Barbara, borrows from the drama of the rocky north as well as the tranquility of the south. Its most rugged and spectacular stretch lies between Monterey and Big Sur. Here is Pebble Beach–where man and nature have joined hands successfully; Big Sur—the most splendid meeting of land and sea; Pt. Lobos—where the delicate balance of nature is carefully protected within a state reserve. Here also is Monterey, once the capital of Spanish California, later a major commercial fishing center. Nearby, Carmel manages to maintain its quaint inner core despite the pressures of tourism.

Around San Luis Obispo, halfway between Monterey and Santa Barbara, are the fog-shrouded fishing villages of Morro Bay and Pismo Beach. But the most notable place in this area is San Simeon, where the Hearst Castle sits high above the town in the Santa Lucia Range.

Below San Luis Obispo, the coast becomes less rugged, the ocean calmer, and the weather warmer. Inland are delightful pockets of green, such as the Ojai Valley, Santa Ynez Valley, and the very Danish community of Solvang. Back at the coast, flower fields at Lompoc and around Ventura add color to the landscape spring to fall.

But the gem of the south-central coast is Santa Barbara, with its splendid setting (nestled between the Pacific Ocean and the Santa Ynez Mountains) and its sparkling, white-washed facade.

Around Monterey Bay

Sherman House, *dating back to 1835, is one of a dozen buildings preserved in Old Monterey. New England seamen arriving in the early 1800s modified the Spanish Colonial architecture to create the Monterey style.*

Yesterday and today *mingle at Monterey's waterfront, where lone pilings (above) and renovated or abandoned buildings recall the once-busy sardine factories immortalized by John Steinbeck in* Cannery Row. *Commercial fishing and processing continue near Fisherman's Wharf (left), where fishmarkets and restaurants keep busy morning to night.*

PHOTOS: TED STRESHINSKY

Spilling *extravagant spring color over Pacific Grove bluffs, ice plant sends roots across most of the Monterey Peninsula's northern coast, warding off erosion.*

Sights along the 17-Mile Drive

PHOTOS: TED STRESHINSKY

Pounding surf *and rocky shores typify the exceptionally scenic stretch of coast along the 17-Mile Drive. The drive also penetrates the pine woods of the Del Monte Forest.*

JACK McDOWELL

It's the complete setting *that makes the Pebble Beach area of the Monterey Peninsula such an outstanding attraction. Ocean-view homes and championship golf courses designed to fit into the landscape enhance the beauty of the scene. The area's three golf courses most famous for their challenging use of ocean and forest (Pebble Beach, Cypress Point, and Spyglass Hill) are the site each January of the Bing Crosby National Pro-Amateur Championship.*

TED STRESHINSKY

Carmel-by-the-Sea...
Carmel Valley

In Carmel-by-the-Sea, *resident artists and craftsmen value the village's simple character—and so do tourists, who crowd shops along Ocean Avenue on weekends.*

In idyllic Carmel Valley, *land that Father Junipero Serra cultivated in 1773 is etched today with fruit orchards and vegetable patches. Where Spanish rancheros once lived and worked, outdoor sports enthusiasts exercise and relax at fine vacation resorts.*

A crescent of powdery sand slopes away from banks of gnarled cypress trees into a hazardous surf at Carmel Beach. A walking beach more than a swimming beach, it's especially pleasant during the early morning or late afternoon.

Fascinating, Fragile Pt. Lobos

Beyond wind-shaped *cypress trees at Point Lobos State Reserve, pelicans and cormorants often roost on Pinnacle Rock, northernmost point in the carefully protected 1,250-acre promontory.*

Happy sea otter *floating nonchalantly offshore is just one of about 1,200 that reside in a coastal reserve from Monterey to 100 miles south. Closer to shore, a low tide exposes a magic land teeming with sea anemones, spiny urchins, mussels, and scuttling hermit crabs (left).*

Aquamarine water *gently washes against the shore in secluded China Cove. A steep staircase braced against the cliff carries walkers to the only beach in Point Lobos safe for swimming.*

Spectacular Big Sur

Off the coast highway, *the mountains and the beaches await exploration. Numerous trails traverse the Ventana Wilderness (right) in the Santa Lucia Mountains, where the southernmost stand of coast redwoods grows. Down at Pfeiffer Beach (below), the chilly water, foamy breakers, and rocky outcroppings attract some swimmers but more beachcombers.*

Big Sur's *wild and rocky landscape rises almost vertically out of the Pacific Ocean into the Santa Lucias. Along the jagged shoreline, the Rocky Creek Bridge on spectacular Highway 1 arches 260 feet over the water.*

RON COHEN

TED STRESHINSKY

A Fishing Village and a Castle of European Treasures

Between ocean runs, *fishing vessels rest in fog-shrouded Morro Bay. The variety of fishing makes this seaside village popular. You can dig for clams during low tide, pick oysters during the March Festival, cast for perch and flounder from piers and jetties, or try for bigger stakes offshore. At the entrance to Morro Bay looms 576-foot Morro Rock.*

Crowning "The Enchanted Hill" *above San Simeon is Hearst Castle, the seaside estate of publishing giant William Randolph Hearst from 1922 to 1951. Now a state historical monument, the mansion and its gardens are open to public touring. Within the main house and the three guest homes are 146 rooms filled with Old World treasures and portions of buildings disassembled in Europe and shipped to San Simeon to be reassembled at the "ranch" (such as the poolside Greek temple shown at left). Hearst even imported his own zoo. Some of the animals, such as zebras, Barbary sheep, and white deer continue to roam in the Santa Lucias.*

Spanish Santa Barbara

El Paseo *shopping arcade, built in and around historic adobes and flagstone courtyards, preserves a flavor reminiscent of Old Spain.*

Classical-Spanish *"Queen of the Missions" reflects remarkable skill and devotion of a handful of padres who, with a few tools, simple materials, and Indian labor, built Mission Santa Barbara in 1815.*

GLENN CHRISTIANSEN

CRAIG AURNESS

One of the most beautiful *civic buildings in the country, Santa Barbara's County Court House resembles a Spanish-Moorish castle, with its red-tiled roof, hand-carved doors, wrought-iron balconies, and tiled corridors.*

Coastal Santa Barbara

Lying between the shores *of a gently curving bay and the Santa Ynez Mountains, Santa Barbara was "La Tierra Adorada"—the beloved land—to Spaniards who settled here in the late 1700s.*

ROY MURPHY

PHOTOS: BOB EVANS

Pelicans and sea lions—and, in the winter, bright coreopsis—are the chief inhabitants of Anacapa, a ragged island in the string of Channel Islands across the channel from Santa Barbara.

Peaceful Valleys
Beyond Santa Barbara

A Danish aura *permeates Solvang, a pocket of Scandinavian charm in the Santa Ynez Valley. Danish-Americans founded the village in 1911 and intentionally built Old World heritage into picturesque windmills, thatched-roof buildings, and culinary culture.*

Lush and orderly *farmlands blanket the Ojai Valley, a moon-shaped hollow protected from fog and wind by hills below the Coast Range. Indians referred to the dale as "The Nest."*

San Luis Mountain *forms a backdrop to a well-known landmark—Mail Pouch Barn—located just off U.S. Highway 101 on the northern outskirts of San Luis Obispo.*

THE CENTRAL COAST **89**

The Los Angeles Area

PHOTOGRAPH BY CRAIG AURNESS

Los Angeles, the West's largest city, was a late bloomer compared to its northern counterpart. It began as a pueblo in 1781 and remained an isolated village until 1876 when the Southern Pacific and Santa Fe railroads promoted a massive "come to Los Angeles on the train" campaign that attracted some 130,000 settlers. After the land rush quieted down, a wildcat oil discovery in 1892 further enticed migrants to the warm-weather mecca out west. Another big population explosion occurred in the 1940s, when industry began to move in on a large scale.

The Los Angeles area today is a massive urban complex, spreading horizontally to the mountains on the north and east, to the beaches on the west, and to the end of Orange County on the south. L.A. is really a city of cities, with well-known places such as Hollywood, Beverly Hills, Pasadena, Santa Monica, Long Beach, and Anaheim included within it.

Los Angeles and Orange counties hold a wide range of activities for the visitor: Amusement parks, such as Disneyland, offer fine family entertainment; museums range from the Getty estate to the L.A. County Museum of Art. You can see live performances at a variety of theaters—from the outdoor Hollywood Bowl to Shubert Theater in Century City. The beaches—from Zuma in the north to Newport in the south—offer sailing, swimming, surfing, and sunning; and the mountains put wilderness at L.A.'s back door.

Placing all of these activities within easy reach of Angeleños is the intricate web of freeways that connect the entire Los Angeles area.

Reminders of Early L.A.

In the Pueblo, *heart of old Los Angeles, Olvera Street (below) evokes the feeling of a Mexican village, with its open booths, bright confusion of goods, and colorful festivities (left).*

Old Plaza Fire House, *on Los Angeles Street with City Hall behind, belonged to Engine Company No. 1 in the late 1800s. Inside (on display) is a horse-drawn fire engine, one of the first used in L.A.*

Early landowners *built Spanish-style homes to suit the Mediterranean climate of Los Angeles. An excellent example is Rancho Los Cerritos, in Long Beach. Constructed in 1844 and restored in 1930, this magnificent hacienda has thick adobe walls, verandas for shade, a central patio, and its original garden.*

A Contemporary Look for Downtown L.A.

TOM TRACY

BILL ROSS

Often called "the stairway to nowhere," *the red steel Double Ascension sculpture by Herbert Bayer brings a Bauhaus touch to the Arco Plaza on Figueroa Street. Underneath the plaza lies the city's first subterranean shopping center.*

A striking high-rise skyline *marks more than a decade of change for downtown L.A. In the 1960s construction began on the face lift, resulting in a bold blend of black and white skyscrapers against the horizon. Among these towers are a chain of plazas and public spaces adorned with fountains and sculptures, roof gardens, and shopping malls—some above and some below street level.*

L.A.'s Civic and Cultural Center

Splashing fountains, *tree-shaded walkways, and pocket gardens liven up Los Angeles' center of government. Serving a city of cities, the Civic Center Complex is the largest concentration of public buildings outside Washington, D.C. On a clear day, the tower observation deck of the 32-story City Hall offers a fine view of the "City of Angels."*

CRAIG AURNESS

Marble and black glass
Dorothy Chandler Pavilion (left) glitters for an evening performance. First in the Music Center complex of three theaters, it seats 3,250 for operas, symphonies, musical comedies, and dance productions. The Mark Taper Forum (below) houses more intimate dramatic productions. Connected by a lofty colonnade is the Ahmanson Theater, a spacious 2,000 seat auditorium.

TOM TRACY

South of Downtown

They're off and running—*that's a familiar cry at Hollywood Park. Thoroughbreds race April to July at this Inglewood track.*

The Trojan, *affectionately known as "Tommy," is USC's symbol. Founded in 1876 the University of Southern California is the state's largest private college.*

One man's imagination *and ambition created Watts Towers, a strangely beautiful assemblage of steel and cement studded with glass, tile, pottery, pebbles, and seashells. Sabatino Rodia spent 33 years on this folk art masterpiece.*

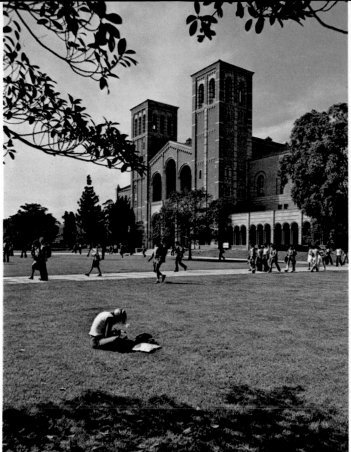

CRAIG AURNESS

West. L.A.

Royce Hall at UCLA *is one of the University's five original Romanesque hilltop buildings. Since 1929 the 411-acre campus has grown into a massive city of learning.*

JERRY FREDRICK

Farmers Market, *a sensory adventure, was started during the depression by 18 farmers who wanted to market their wasting crops. Today it's a sprawling complex of shops, offering everything from irresistible produce to delicatessen-type foods.*

TED STRESHINSKY

Los Angeles County Museum *of Art, housed in three gleaming pavilions, sits atop the La Brea Tar Pits in Hancock Park. Collections range from ancient treasures, Impressionist paintings, and futuristic experiments to sculpture exhibited in the garden.*

Century City *rises boldly near the junction of two beautiful boulevards—Wilshire and Santa Monica. A city within a city, it was once Tom Mix's ranch, then a studio lot, and now an architectural showcase.*

Highlights of Movieland

At Universal Studios, *daredevil stuntmen perform amazing feats for visitors. The studio's main attraction, a 2-hour tram tour, shows the sound stages, labs, dressing rooms, and action on the 420-acre back lot.*

JERRY FREDRICK

Hand, foot, and hoof *prints of the stars in concrete in front of Mann's (long known as Grauman's) Chinese Theatre trace the history of Hollywood cinema since the theatre's opening in 1927.*

CRAIG AURNESS

Summer crowds *at the Hollywood Bowl listen to the popular "Symphonies under the Stars." Once a simple bandstand in the middle of a weedy dell in the Cahuenga Hills, the bowl today is a complex amphitheater seating 17,400. Reasons for the bowl's success are its natural setting, good acoustics, and fine musical programs.*

THE LOS ANGELES AREA **103**

Mammoth Griffith Park, *in its 4,000 acres, offers something for everyone. Along its perimeter, flatlands provide plenty of room for picnics, tennis, swimming, and impromptu sports. Its mountainous heartland presents hiking challenges.*

Travel Town, *in the park's northeast corner, contains the West's largest collection of rail equipment. You can poke around or walk through retired locomotives, cabooses, and streetcars.*

Super Griffith Park

High on a hill, *Griffith Observatory commands a spectacular panorama of the city at night. The large dome houses a planetarium; smaller domes contain telescopes. On display are a Foucault pendulum and a model of the visible side of the moon.*

Bighorn sheep *and mountain goats perch comfortably atop rocky heights at the Los Angeles Zoo. On 110 acres, over 2,000 animals reside in settings similar to their natural habitat.*

Riding stables *front on Riverside Drive, one of the park's boundaries. Forty-three miles of bridle trails wind through the highlands and lowlands of Griffith Park.*

Around Malibu...
A Roman Villa,
an Expanse of Beach

Zuma Beach, *off the coast highway north of Malibu, is effectively separated from its neighboring beach to the south by Pt. Dume, a sandstone finger. Rolling dunes flow down to a good swimming beach at Zuma, L.A.'s largest county-owned strand.*

PHOTOS: TED STRESHINSKY

JACK McDOWELL

The J. Paul Getty Museum, *replica of an ancient Roman villa, houses a treasure of Greek and Roman statuary, Louis XV and XVI furniture, rare tapestries, and paintings by Dutch and Italian masters. Upon his death in 1976, the "world's richest man" left the bulk of his estate to the museum.*

Around crescent-shaped *Santa Monica Bay is a series of beaches, each with its own special appeal. Santa Monica, busiest of the bay's beaches, draws sunbathers and swimmers to its wide, sandy shore.*

BILL ROSS

BILL ROSS

Santa Monica Bay: L.A.'s Aquatic Playground

From Santa Monica Beach, *a shoreline of high-rises comes into view. Here, and at Redondo Beach just to the south, a carnival of activities takes place along the piers.*

JERRY FREDRICK

Warm weather *and water temperatures combine to attract thousands of Angeleños to the beach each year. On mild summer evenings, body surfers linger long after dusk.*

Sailing vessels *of all sizes ply the channel or head out to sea from Marina del Rey, largest manmade pleasure boat harbor on the West Coast. Shoreside amenities include shops, marina services, and luxury condominiums.*

Wayfarer's Chapel, *an imaginative combination of glass walls and redwood beams, sits high above Portuguese Bend on the Palos Verdes Peninsula. Designed by Lloyd Wright, son of the famous architect, the chapel opened in 1949 to worshipers of all faiths.*

Hang glider *rides the air currents near Pt. Fermin State Park in San Pedro. From the park are fine views toward Catalina. On the point stands a lighthouse, built in 1874 of wood brought around Cape Horn.*

Rugged Palos Verdes Peninsula

For about 15 miles, *the rocky bluffs of the Palos Verdes Peninsula interrupt the flat sandy beaches of Los Angeles County. An exceptionally scenic drive winds around the peninsula, through beautiful residential areas and past points of interest, such as Marineland of the Pacific. Overlooks provide views of a sea-carved shoreline.*

Catalina–
A Summer
Destination
for Angeleños

Avalon Bay (right) is the boat tourist's first view of Catalina. Lying 21 miles offshore, the island is a mountain range split by a low isthmus, as rugged as the islands of Greece. The island's only city, Avalon (below) has been welcoming vacationers since 1887.

PHOTOS: JERRY FREDRICK

Clear water, *equable climate, and pure air lure sun and water worshipers to Catalina. You can reach the island via excursion or private boat, amphibians, or turbojets that land at the island's "airport in the sky."*

THE LOS ANGELES AREA **113**

Pasadena...Home of the Rose Bowl

BILL ROSS

Spectators jam *the stands and overflow onto the curbs to watch the colorful New Year's Day Parade of Roses. Entries in the procession along Colorado Boulevard include riding groups, marching bands, and flower-decorated floats— all vying for coveted awards.*

On New Year's Day, *some 100,000 fans gather at Rose Bowl Stadium for the football classic between the "Pac 10" and "Big 10" champions. During the rest of the year, the stadium holds swap meets, political rallies, and civic events.*

The Norton Simon Museum of Art, *with its cornerless tile-clad exterior, symbolizes a new look for Pasadena. Museum highlights include a collection of 20th-century art and a sculpture garden.*

Gamble House, *designed by Greene and Greene and built in 1908, had a design so original and so well adapted to the locale that it spread throughout California. Emphasis was on integrated indoor/outdoor living.*

Architectural
Statements
in Pasadena

Grand and ornate *City Hall, built
in the 1920s during a revival of Spanish
architecture, stands with the Civic
Auditorium and Library along a short
stretch of Garfield Avenue.*

PHOTOS: CRAIG AURNESS

The 200-acre Huntington estate *in San
Marino is known for its outstanding
Library, Art Gallery, and Botanical
Gardens. In the formal rose gardens
stands this small temple, originally
from a French estate.*

Surprises in the San Gabriels

Forming the northern border *for Los Angeles, the San Gabriels are often called L.A.'s backyard mountain playground. From the Angeles Crest Highway, the wrinkled and gently contoured mountains may seem uninviting to the casual visitor, but hiking trails lead to streams, waterfalls, canyons, a variety of vegetation, and spectacular views.*

Every season *reveals a special scenic delight in the San Gabriels. All you have to do is leave the highway for a short hike. Wildflowers peek shyly from a grassy nook in spring, dry weeds form their own arrangements in fall, and a pristine cape of snow blankets high ground in winter.*

PHOTOS: TED STRESHINSKY

Highest of the mountain ranges *surrounding Los Angeles, the San Bernardinos are a part of the mountain barrier between the coast and desert. Here peaks are tall—Mt. San Gorgonio rises up to 11,052 feet, with many others on the south face reaching over 10,000 feet. Tucked into the mountains are recreation areas and some rugged wilderness. Scenic Rim of the World Drive winds through the heart of the San Bernardinos between 5,000 and 7,200 feet.*

In the San Bernardinos, High above L.A.

PHOTOS: ROY MURPHY

Lake Arrowhead, *manmade recreation lake and an all-year resort, lies off the Rim of the World highway. Boating activities prevail in summer, skiing in winter. At the south end of the lake is a picturesque alpine-style village. Around the lake, vacation homes lie hidden among pines and cedars.*

Disneyland on Parade

BILL ROSS

TOM TRACY

The "Mark Twain," *a main attraction in Frontierland, passes Tom Sawyer's island on a cruise down the river. Across the river is Ft. Wilderness, a haunt of Davy Crockett.*

Multicolored fireworks *explode on summer nights at 9 p.m., illuminating Sleeping Beauty's Castle—across the moat at the entrance to Fantasyland.*

Monorail glides *quietly around the park's perimeter offering a passing glance at other attractions before crossing over to Disneyland Hotel.*

CRAIG AURNESS

The Disneyland Parade *(above), a spectacle of showmanship, passes down Main Street, 1890, Home Town, USA. Father of the theme parks cropping up all over the country, Disneyland was designed to delight adults as well as children. Within its 65 acres are four make-believe lands—Adventureland, Frontierland, Fantasyland, and Tomorrowland—where technology and imagination are put to use to control the environment and achieve illusion. Trams giving visitors an aerial view of the park pass through the Matterhorn (left)—Disney's answer to a roller coaster and one of the park's most popular rides.*

THE LOS ANGELES AREA **123**

San Juan Capistrano's mission, *founded in 1776 by Father Junipero Serra, attracts visitors as well as swallows. The legendary swallows arrive every year on March 19 (around St. Josephs Day) and leave October 23 (date of the death of the mission's patron saint).*

TOM TRACY

More Orange County Attractions

Stripes and checks *are fashionable at Lion Country Safari, a 500-acre wild animal park south of Irvine. Here animals roam freely, while visitors are "caged" in cars.*

PHOTOS: CRAIG AURNESS

From a roadside stand *in a berry patch in the 1920s, Knott's Berry Farm has grown into a 200-acre family entertainment center, with rides (left), shops, restaurants, a theater, and a "ghost town." A brick replica of Philadelphia's Independence Hall (above) stands at the entrance.*

Surfing, Sailing, Shopping the Orange County Coast

Newport Bay—*with its opulent waterfront homes, yacht clubs, and mast-studded harbor—has little to do with the past when it was simply a "new port" between San Diego and San Pedro. Although Newport's attractions are still at the beach, the town has expanded beyond its elegant waterfront, with housing developments, a financial complex, and a huge shopping center.*

Balboa Island's *short 3-block shopping district is jammed during the summer. The most interesting—but not the fastest— way over to the island is by ferry from Balboa Peninsula.*

"Surf's up," *a familiar cry at Huntington Beach, brings boys and boards to ride some of the coast's greatest combers. Most of the activity along the incredibly long beach, site of the summer international surfing competition, centers around Huntington Pier.*

San
Diego

PHOTOGRAPH BY JACK McDOWELL

An equable climate and splendid bay setting have attracted so many people to San Diego that it now ranks as California's second largest city. These same attributes have also made the city a year-round vacation destination.

San Diego grew up around its crescent-shaped bay. Protected from ocean surges by natural breakwaters, San Diego Bay provides shelter for a variety of boats—from Navy destroyers to commercial fishing vessels and pleasure craft.

Modern planning has turned California's southernmost city into a recreational boating paradise. Along Shelter and Harbor islands, two manmade islands jutting out into San Diego Bay, there are marinas, hotels, and restaurants catering to tourism. Boating channels, islands, sheltered coves, sandy beaches and trim marinas teem with activity in 4,600-acre Mission Bay, formerly a dismal tidal flat. More San Diego attractions include Balboa Park, home of the fine San Diego Zoo; Mission San Diego Alcala, first in the long chain of California Missions; and Pt. Loma, where the first European landed in California in 1542.

Beyond San Diego's city limits are more enticements. Mountains and desert lie east of town, to the north are the seaside village of La Jolla and the rare Torrey pines, and to the south are colorful Mexican border towns.

Handsome Serra Museum *atop Presidio Hill over-looks Old Town San Diego State Historic Park. Once the site of California's first mission, it now houses exhibits from Spanish days and provides excellent sunset city views.*

California's "Old Town"

ED COOPER

Mission San Diego *de Alcala's campanile adds a striking touch to its graceful facade. The "Mother of the Missions" has Sunday services and museum tours.*

A tribute *to California's first "city," 6½-block-long Old Town is a combination of old and new San Diego. Best seen on foot, it offers shopping in nostalgic emporiums (right), tours of restored adobes, and dining (below) in a colorful Mexican restaurant in Bazaar del Mundo.*

San Diego Bay...
Busy with Business
and Recreation

San Diego's skyline *presents a postcard view from the southwest side of San Diego Bay. Jutting out into the bay are two manmade islands—Shelter (foreground) and Harbor. Lined with marinas, hotels, and restaurants, they cater to residents and vacationers attracted to San Diego's mild year-round climate and splendid bayside setting.*

In port *along the Embarcadero, tuna crewmen keep busy sorting and mending nets. The largest fishing fleet in the United States leaves San Diego to seine for tuna as far south as Chile.*

PHOTOS: JACK McDOWELL

Naval vessels *moored along Harbor Drive host open house one weekend a month. Around San Diego the Navy is everywhere—from submarine pens and fueling depots on Point Loma to the Air Station on Coronado's North Island and the mothball fleet moored in the south bay.*

Colorful sailboats *dot Mission Bay's blue waters. Twenty years of dredging and development turned this bleak estuary into a 4,600-acre aquatic playground (viewed below from the tower at Vacation Village), featuring islands, lagoons, beaches, golf courses, and vacation resorts.*

Mission Bay... from Estuary to Vast Vacationland

At Sea World, *in Mission Bay, an agile black and white killer whale usually steals the show. There are water exhibitions, aquarium displays, and Japanese pearl divers; you can ride a hydrofoil on the water or an aerial tram above the water.*

Casa del Prado, *a memorial to the 1915 Panama-California International Exposition, forms the nucleus of the park's cultural scene. The idea of this grand park dates back to 1874 when the city fathers acquired 1,400 acres of open, hilly chaparral "to be a park forever."*

Balboa Park... Oasis in the Heart of Town

Diversity *is the key to the park's popularity. Within its attractively landscaped area are hiking trails, lawn bowling courts, balloons signaling entry to the 128-acre zoo, and live entertainment at the Old Globe Theater.*

San Diego's Delightful Animal World

Pelican Blacksmith plovers

Indian elephants

Siberian tiger

Congo peacock

Okapi

Lioness

San Diego Wild Animal Park *is home to some 2,000 animals and birds, many rare and endangered. On 1,800 acres in the San Pasqual Valley 30 miles north of downtown San Diego, animals roam chaparral terrain resembling Africa's dry, upland plains. You view the action from a 5-mile monorail ride or from a short nature walk. The parent zoo in Balboa Park allows you to get closer to the animals.*

Victorian Elegance on Coronado

Sweeping span *of the Coronado-San Diego bridge rises high above San Diego Bay. Designed with low guard rails, the bridge affords panoramic views from the San Diego skyline south into Mexico. Before completion of the bridge in 1969, ferry boats were the only way to reach Coronado Island.*

Sprawling in Victorian splendor, *Hotel del Coronado is a San Diego architectural wonder and a state historic landmark. Picturesque boathouse (now a restaurant) rests at the edge of Glorietta Bay, a small boat harbor. Of later vintage, its design matches that of the hotel.*

ED COOPER

Pt. Loma, *the high promontory that shelters San Diego Bay from the Pacific Ocean, attracts visitors for spectacular city and coastline views. On the point, a statue of Juan Cabrillo stands, facing the actual spot where he landed his vessel in 1542. Cabrillo is credited with the discovery of California.*

At the Tip of San Diego

Trim lighthouse *atop Pt. Loma guided sailors for 37 years. In 1891 the light, frequently obscured by clouds, was moved down to the water's edge.*

Pounding waves *at Shadow Cliffs batter the point, foaming across and often eroding the rock. This is the meeting place of San Diego Bay and the Pacific Ocean.*

Seaside North of San Diego

La Jolla's seashore—*with coves, caves, cliffs, and beaches for swimming, diving, surfing, tidepool exploring, and walking—has been attracting vacationers since 1886. But, there's more to La Jolla than its celebrated waterfront. Scripps Institution of Oceanography and the Salk Institute for Biological Studies make it a center for research.*

BILL ROSS

Large Torrey pine, *silhouetted by the sunset, grows only along the coast north of La Jolla and at Santa Rosa Island 195 miles away. Protected now in a state reserve, these trees stood when Cabrillo sighted land in 1542.*

Sleek thoroughbreds *work out at the beach every morning during the summer preparing to race at Del Mar, often called the world's most beautiful track.*

Road between Banner and Julian, *two former gold mining towns, climbs from desert into mountains. The highway, winding its sinuous corkscrew course along Banner Grade, affords fine views of peaceful agricultural valleys.*

San Diego's Back Country

Venerable barn *in Aguanga serves as a reminder of the past when this town was a way station on the famous Butterfield Stage line between St. Louis and San Francisco.*

Pastoral Santa Ysabel *reflects on its history. A mission outpost, built in 1818, welcomes visitors; the old general store dates from 1870.*

California's Desert

Although California is generally thought of as seashore and mountains, rolling hills and valleys, one-fifth of the state is covered by desert. This vast and lonely expanse of land stretches from Los Angeles and San Diego east to the Colorado River, from the end of the Central Valley south to Mexico, and north along the Sierra's eastern flank.

Arid conditions make the desert environment unlike any other in the state. There are no rushing streams, tranquil lakes, dense forests, lush valleys, crashing waves. But the desert has a qualitative beauty all its own...shifting sand dunes, mountains boldly sculptured by abrasive winds and flash floods, and exposed soil in magnificent shades of reds, browns, blacks, and yellows that are transformed by a haze of distance into magentas, blues, and purples.

One state park and two national monuments make getting acquainted with the desert in its natural state possible. Highlights of Anza-Borrego State Park are sharply eroded badlands and low desert vegetation. Within Joshua Tree National Monument are intriguing rock formations and plants and animals native to both high and low desert. Death Valley National Monument contains salt plains, sand dunes, craters, and mountains peaking at 11,049 feet.

Man has tamed part of the desert. Around Palm Springs, residents live the year around in air-conditioned comfort while vacationers flock to the resorts to soak up the winter sun. And thousands of acres of wasteland in the Imperial and Coachella valleys have been reclaimed by irrigation to produce a variety of crops.

Anza-Borrego: A Vast Expanse of Untamed Desert

Carrizo badlands *leave an indelible impression on the desert traveler, for the sharply eroded mud hills stretch for miles before fading into the distant horizon. In addition to these sunbaked wastelands, Anza-Borrego Desert State Park contains within its nearly half a million acres about 600 native plant species, a showy display of spring wildflowers, bighorn sheep, and fine stands of California fan palms and elephant trees.*

JACK McDOWELL

Smoke trees, *common to dry sandy washes, are so named because their almost leafless and thorny blue-grey twigs look like wisps of smoke. Purple-blue pea-shaped flowers appear after spring rains.*

Desert washes, *created and nurtured by flash floods and soil erosion, twist in labyrinthine patterns across Anza-Borrego. Sometimes they are lined with desert willows and smoke trees.*

Recreation and Reclamation in the Desert

JACK McDOWELL

JAMES H. FLANAGAN

With irrigation and imagination, *man has learned to transform the desert's sandy wastes into fertile land. At the turn of the century, the Coachella Valley was simply a part of the Colorado Desert. Today it's a 55,000-acre garden plot, famous for date palms and citrus groves.*

East of the San Jacinto Mountains *lies the Palm Springs oasis. Here, in the "Golf Capital of the World," the winter weary congregate to take advantage of the excellent resort facilities and the warm, dry desert climate. In February, peak of the season, Palm Desert courses provide the setting for the Bob Hope Desert Classic.*

Straddling Southern California's *two great deserts, the low Colorado and the high Mojave, is Joshua Tree National Monument. The reserve demonstrates the full range of desert environments, from lowland (up to 3,000 feet) to highland.*

In Joshua Tree, High Desert and Low Desert

Shaggy brown limbs *and stiff pointed leaves characterize the curious plant that gave Joshua Tree National Monument its name. In March or April, these desert members of the lily family bloom with showy clusters of greenish-white flowers.*

PHOTOS: ED COOPER

Jumping cholla *grow knee-high across low deserts but penetrate transition zones as well. The plant's waxy yellow flowers appear at branch tips in April.*

Early morning and late afternoon sunlight *cast softening shadows across Death Valley's huge expanse (14 square miles) of sand dunes. During the cool hours of the day, the dunes are most inviting. Footprints don't mar the surface long, for the powerful desert winds blow the sand smooth or into delicate ripples and dramatic waves. Growing green on the dunes are creosote bushes, among the most common plants in the Great American Desert.*

Death Valley's Dramatic Dunes

Sandy faces *of the dunes constantly change under the forces of the shifting winds, but their main contours remain unchanged year after year.*

PHOTOS: TED STRESHINSKY

Death Valley...
Desert with a
Difference

At Devil's Golfcourse, *coral-like spires and ridges of almost pure sodium chloride jut up two feet. This intriguing work of nature is part of the valley floor's immense sea of salt.*

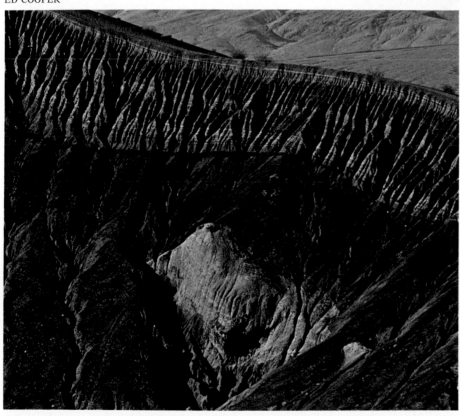

Ubehebe Crater, *a result of volcanic activity, lies on the north side of Death Valley. Some 3,000 years ago, hot gases beneath Ubehebe exploded, covering the countryside for miles with black dust and cinders. This violent activity produced the massive crater 750 feet deep and one-half mile wide at the top.*

Snow-crowned Telescope Peak *(11,049 feet) and brackish Badwater reflect Death Valley's elevation extremes. Lowest point in the Western Hemisphere, 282 feet below sea level, lies just beyond Badwater.*

Brilliantly colored Artist's Palette *is a mixture of eroded rocks, volcanic lava, and mud and gravel exposed by repeated faulting of the Black Mountains. Oxidation of mineral-bearing ores produces the exquisite reds, pinks, oranges, purples, yellows, and greens—all intensified by the light of the setting sun. You see Artist's Palette about halfway along the 9½-mile Artist's Drive.*

Death Valley... a Kaleidoscope

PHOTOS: TED STRESHINSKY

Superbly carved Funeral Mountains, *as viewed from Zabriskie Point, are the result of millions of years of faulting, uplifting, and erosion. The best time to view this spectacular sight is exactly at sunrise, when the light creates patterns of shadows and shows the earthy browns at their best.*

The Desert's Colorful Carpet

Beaver Tail

Mound Cactus

Evening-Primrose

Desert-Aster

Blazing Star

Prickly-Pear

A mass of brilliant color *blankets the desert in spring when wildflowers burst into bloom. Winter rains followed by sunny days trigger germination, and, within a few months, an array of plants—from cactus to splashy desert dandelions (right)—blossom on alluvial fans and along gravelly washes. To survive the climatic desert extremes, native plants have evolved a variety of defenses. Light-colored leaves and stems reflect sunlight, small leaves reduce loss of water, and leaf pores close during the heat of the day.*

BETTY RANDALL

Owens Valley–in the Shadow of the Sierra

JACK McDOWELL

Alabama Hills *stand at the base of the sheer eastern face of the Sierra Nevada. Millions of years ago this jumble of rocks broke away from the Sierra and lodged in the valley below. Sagebrush and tumbleweed cover much of the Owens Valley, since clouds are drained of moisture as they pass over the crest of the range.*

Fremont cottonwoods *brighten up the Bishop area when their leaves turn a lemon yellow in fall. Most of the Owens Valley is too dry for farming, but about 19,000 acres are irrigated for alfalfa and pasture.*

Tule elk, *world's smallest and rarest elk, roam the range between Big Pine and Independence. Native to the Central Valley, their population dwindled as farms replaced grassland. In the 1930s, 27 elk were resettled in the Owens Valley. By the early 1970s, their population numbered 340.*

East of the Sierra: the Prehistoric and Historic

Eccentric statues *rising in bizarre patterns six to ten feet above the water of Mono Lake are tufa deposits. For centuries the soft, porous rock has been forming from chemicals carried to the lake by streams.*

ED COOPER

BETTY RANDALL

Weathered survivors *slowly rot in Bodie, once one of the most raucous gold mining towns in the West. Bodie boomed in 1859, boasting 10,000 people, 67 saloons, and reportedly a murder a day. Now a true ghost town, Bodie's buildings stand protected in "arrested decay" in a state park.*

More than 4,000 years *of harsh weather have shaped the tenacious bristlecone pines, oldest living trees on earth. They grow on barren slopes of the White Mountains above 10,000 feet.*

The Sierra Nevada

From a distance the Sierra Nevada, with its magnificent meringuelike peaks, looks forbidding and impenetrable. But, to those who know the range first-hand, the Sierra is a hospitable world of crystal clear lakes, rushing streams, spectacular waterfalls, dense forests, steep-walled canyons, and exquisite meadows.

The largest single mountain mass in the country, the Sierra Nevada (Spanish for snowy range) rises gradually from the floor of the Central Valley, reaching heights of from 7,000 to 14,495 feet before dropping almost vertically into the Owens Valley and Nevada plateau on the east. As the Sierra stretches from north to south for about 400 miles, the range gains in elevation, with the southern Sierra the true High Sierra.

Certain places are instantly associated with the Sierra. Lake Tahoe, in the northern part, sparkles in the midst of pine and fir forests. In the central Sierra, Yosemite National Park has within its boundaries the highlights of the range: a glacially carved valley, feathery and thunderous waterfalls, massive cliffs of granite, and fine subalpine meadows. Sequoia and Kings Canyon national parks, in the southern Sierra, contain native stands of giant sequoias, the sharply chiseled Kaweah Peaks, and Mt. Whitney—at 14,495 feet the highest mountain in the continental United States outside Alaska.

In addition to the well-visited and well-known spots, the Sierra Nevada offers its magnificent, abundant wilderness, waiting to be explored and enjoyed by those willing, able, and prepared to step off the well-trodden path. Here are perhaps the real joys of the Sierra, where they can be cherished in solitude.

Lake Tahoe– A Year-round Recreational Mecca

DICK ROWAN

In winter, *thousands of skiers glide down snow-clad slopes at Tahoe, California's major ski center. At Heavenly Valley, on the south shore, ski runs provide commanding views of the incredibly blue lake.*

TOM TRACY

Emerald Bay, *with the lake beyond, lies near the south end of Tahoe's 71-mile shoreline drive. All along the lake, you'll find vistas like this, where granite cliffs plummet to the water. Along the shore are pebble or sand beaches fringed with pines and cedar. This "Jewel of the Sierra," 22 miles long and 8 to 12 miles wide, has plenty of room for powerboats, water-skiers, and fishermen. Many miles of back country trails await the hiker.*

Yosemite National Park: A Monument to Nature

TED STRESHINSKY

Awesome view *of Yosemite Valley from Inspiration Point near the Wawona Tunnel gives visitors an excellent idea of how glaciers carved the valley. During the Ice Age, glaciers advanced and receded three times, finally leaving a U-shaped valley and distinguished landmarks, such as (from left to right) El Capitan, Cloud's Rest, Half Dome, and Cathedral Rocks.*

Rafts float *calmly on beyond a bridge over this placid stretch of the Merced River. Mountain creeks cascade into the valley, join to flow gently for a while, then plunge down to the low country.*

PHOTOS: TED STRESHINSKY

Grassy meadows *and woodlands of fir, pines, oak, dogwood, and buckeye cover the valley floor. At the end of the Ice Age, melting glaciers formed a lake here. Thousands of years of silting produced the rich and level soils where these hikers wade in meadow grass.*

Yosemite Valley– Mountains, Meadows, and Waterfalls

Best way *to view Yosemite's natural beauty is to bike valley roads or hike trails that crisscross the flat ground and lead into the high country. Mist Trail, a 1.4-mile hike from the valley floor, offers a closeup—and wet—view of Vernal Falls' spectacular drop and of granite exquisitely polished by glaciers (left).*

HARALD SUND

The "Old Faithfuls" of Yosemite Valley

Incomparable Yosemite Falls *cascades 1,430 feet down to a rocky obstacle course before beginning its final 1,000-foot thunderous descent to the valley floor. Fed by snowmelt, the falls are at their splashiest in late spring, are reduced to a trickle in late summer.*

RUSSELL LAMB

El Capitan, *said to be the largest single block of granite in the world, never surrendered to glacial power. Its hard rock proved too strong for the ice to move.*

Most distinctive landmark *in the valley is Half Dome, looming 4,800 feet above the valley floor. This monolithic gray rock grows smaller every year, for granite debris falls away from its legendary "tear-stained" face.*

The John Muir Trail– from Tuolumne Meadows to Mt.Whitney

TED STRESHINSKY

JACK McDOWELL

Tuolumne Meadows, *in Yosemite's high country, is the starting point for the 212-mile-long John Muir Trail. Near the trail head, you'll find many walk-in campsites and good fishing amid the finest scenery Yosemite can offer.*

High above timberline, *the John Muir Trail ends at 14,495-foot Mt. Whitney, highest point in the continental United States outside Alaska. From Trail Crest Pass, elevation 13,777 feet, the view is of a harsh, moody, and beautiful landscape—one etched with ragged peaks, fluted cliffs, and glacially gouged valleys.*

Sierra Lakes and Streams...
Plentiful and Serene

About 1,500 lakes—*ranging from tiny pools to 22-mile-long Lake Tahoe—lie along the Sierra's western slope. You'll find many at mid-elevation (such as Bear Lake, below, in Emigrant Wilderness), but glacial activity has made the High Sierra a "land of lakes." Most of these tranquil pockets of blue are hidden from all but backpackers.*

Tremendous snowpack *on the Sierra's western side nourishes streams, flora, and fauna. Spring's warming temperatures trigger snowmelt.*

JACK McDOWELL

Delightful mountain streams *support an incredible variety of plant and animal life, such as sedges, algae, mosses, wild onions, corn lilies, mayflys, and trout.*

Springtime in the Sierra

Alpine gentian

Snow plant

Indian paintbrush

Bitterroot

Leopard Lily

Fremont's Xerasid

Sky pilot

Sierra spring *extends from May to July. As warm days melt the snow pack, the meadows turn green, streams are full, and wildflowers begin to bloom. More than 550 kinds of wildflowers grow here. They come in a rainbow of colors, and, depending on species and elevation, blossom from April through October.*

High in the Sierra... Traces of an Ice Age

TOM TRACY

Devils Postpile, *a 60-foot-high mass of basalt prisms, was formed from cooling lava after nearby Mammoth Mountain erupted some 915,000 years ago. It was then bared to view when glaciers carved out the valley.*

ED COOPER

As glaciers moved *through the mountains, they polished and cracked some rocks, dislodged and carried along others. Resulting erratics (vagrant chunks of granite) were left stranded when the ice finally receded.*

Second Lake, *below the Palisade Glacier, gets its milky green color from "glacial flour," fine silt left from passing ice. In the Sierra today, about 60 small glaciers not more than 4,000 years old sit in northeast hollows of the highest peaks.*

Miniature world *of grasses and wild-flowers has its roots in the shallow soil of high-country meadows. Because of the two-month growing season, the ecological balance of life in these alpine meadows is extremely fragile.*

Most of the true *High Sierra lies within Kings Canyon and Sequoia national parks, between the sharply chiseled Kaweah Peaks on the west (below) and the Sierra crest on the east.*

PHOTOS: RANDY MORGENSON

In Sequoia and Kings Canyon, Glories of Nature

Giant sequoias (Sequoiadendron giganteum), *preserved within Kings Canyon and Sequoia national parks, are the largest trees in the world. But, it's more than size that makes the "Big Trees" so awesome . . . it's their mystical quality and striking beauty.*

The Rocky World of the High Sierra

PHOTOS: TED STRESHINSKY

Surprises *await the visitor to the alpine world of the High Sierra. Although the landscape looks desolate and uninviting, you'll find hidden valleys and forests, lush meadows, rushing streams, peaceful lakes, signs of past and present life, and sweeping panoramas that you must see to believe.*

Gold Rush Country

When James Marshall discovered a few flakes of gold dust in the mill-race of Captain Sutter's sawmill along the American River in 1848, the attention of the world turned to California. During the next few years, hordes of gold-seekers converged on the Sierra Nevada foothills, leaving an impression on the land that remains more than a century later.

Many changes have occurred since the frantic days of the Gold Rush. One-time boom towns have vanished under lakes or have been destroyed by fire. Others are marked only by skeletal headframes or piles of rubble. A few have become prosperous towns, with only traces of the past peeking from beneath a modern facade.

Fortunately some of the area's unique character lingers. Historic buildings (especially in Coloma and Columbia state historic parks) have been preserved and given new life. Antique shops display samples of the past, and charming inns (renovated hotels or houses) offer old-fashioned hospitality.

Unfortunately, in their enthusiasm to "strike it rich," the Forty-Niners and their followers left many a scar on the landscape. The most obvious resulted from hydraulic mining, a more economical means of mining than panning, sluicing, or dredging. With water under pressure directed at soft gravels, mountain ridges disintegrated. At Malakoff Diggins, scene of the biggest hydraulic mining operation in the world, time has softened the wounds.

PHOTOGRAPH BY JACK McDOWELL

Remnants of the "Rush"

Silent sentinels *recall many a collapsed dream. At Pilot Hill stands lonely "Bayley's Folly" (above). Built in 1862 as a hotel, it remains without a purpose because the Central Pacific railroad changed its route. Tombstones, like those at Mokelumne Hill (right), mark final resting places for many miners who never struck it rich.*

Relics of a golden era *dot the Mother Lode. The Kennedy Mine headframe (above), towering over former mining headquarters and ore-carrying trestles, dominates the countryside around Jackson. Huge tailing wheels used for waste disposal still stand along the Jackson Gate Road. Weathered wagon (left) outside Amador City might have traveled the side road to Drytown—through one-time Bunker Hill, New Philadelphia, and New Chicago.*

WILLIAM CARTER

Columbia's collection *of reconstructed buildings and mining artifacts make it a show place for the Gold Country. Once dubbed the Gem of the Southern Mines, it is now a state historic park, offering a wealth of activities for family fun (panning for gold, riding a stagecoach, sipping sarsaparilla at the saloon, dining at historic Columbia House, or watching a performance at Fallon House).*

Historic Columbia and Coloma

In Coloma, *the first gold boom town, you can visit a replica of Sutter's sawmill (top) where James Marshall found gold or try your luck panning the American River.*

Malakoff Diggins...
Mining Scar Mellowed by Time

Malakoff's wounds, *testimony to both the effectiveness and destructiveness of hydraulic mining, soften with the passage of time. In quiet North Bloomfield, now part of Malakoff Diggins State Historic Park, are giant monitors (nozzles) that once blasted water to crumble ridge banks for gold.*

198 GOLD RUSH COUNTRY

Tiny St. Sava's *Serbian Orthodox Church and surrounding cemetery in Jackson appear dwarfed by the rising foothills. Built in 1894 this small simple structure is the Orthodox mother church for the entire North American continent.*

19th-Century Architectural Treasures

Red Castle's *ornate exterior dates back to the 1860s. Architecturally typical of Nevada City buildings, this inn sits high atop Prospect Hill overlooking the city.*

PHOTOS: WILLIAM CARTER

Classically simple lines *and stark white walls of Mariposa's two-story wooden courthouse stand just as the builders left them in 1854. Tower clock has tolled the hour since 1866.*

JACK McDOWELL

Bells and acorns *adorn the facade of Sonora's showpiece, an intricately decorated classic built in 1890. Underneath this house run tunnels of the Bonanza Mine, one of the greatest gold pockets ever discovered.*

Far from a ghost town, *Nevada City preserves and restores its venerable structures. Here you can spend a night in an inn, watch a movie in a 19th-century theater, or browse among museums and shops.*

White water *draws rafting enthusiasts every summer to Sierra streams. Although the most accessible rivers to run are the Stanislaus (shown at right) and American, the Tuolumne offers the most exciting ride.*

Gold Country Happenings Today

Mellow inns, *such as the one at Sutter Creek, offer old-fashioned hospitality. Overnight stays in the Gold Country provide extra time for antiquing and for exploring small shops, like those in Amador City (above).*

The Central Valley

Agriculture dominates California's Central Valley, for this valley in the heart of the state is the nation's richest farming area. Over 200 crops yield a multi-billion dollar harvest annually and provide the nation with a substantial percentage of its food.

The Central Valley runs 465 miles from Redding south to Bakersfield. Bounded by the Coast Range on the west and the Sierra Nevada on the east, it varies in width from 30 to 60 miles. Actually the Central Valley unites two smaller valleys, the Sacramento in the north and the San Joaquin in the south, each named for the river that flows through it.

Large-scale water control of the Sacramento and San Joaquin rivers are the key to the Central Valley's agricultural success. Through the Central Valley Project and the California State Water Project, dams, reservoirs, canals, and pumping stations capture and reserve the water, then release and channel it to where it is needed.

Dotting the valley are good-sized cities as well as farming communities. Some, like Visalia and Fresno, grew up with agriculture. Others, like Sacramento and Stockton, were born in the Gold Rush and went on to become major metropolitan areas in their own right. Both Sacramento and Stockton are inland ports, and Sacramento has served as capital of the Golden State since 1854.

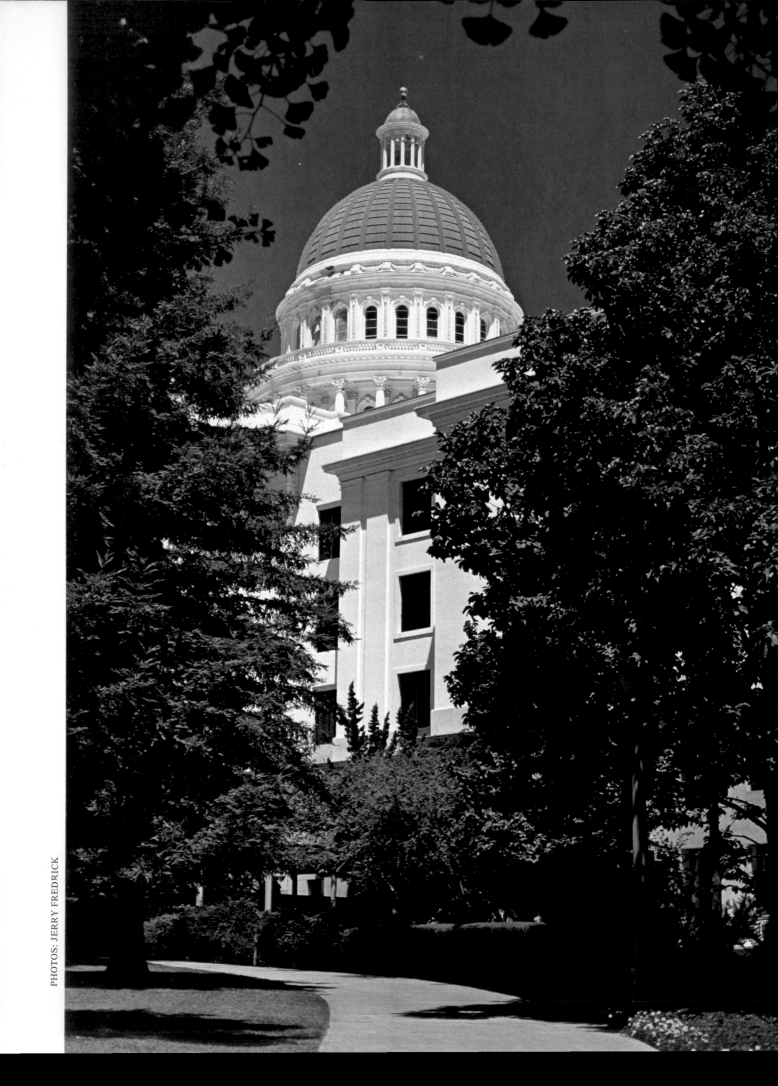

Sacramento– Capital City since 1854

Oldest art museum *in the West, the E. B. Crocker Art Gallery features Oriental and contemporary American works. This elegant Victorian mansion was built by Judge Crocker in 1873 to house his private collection.*

An echo of the good old days *resounds in Old Sacramento, a 28-acre section of town along the waterfront. Restored buildings and plank sidewalks, wagons and "watering holes" recapture the colorful atmosphere of the 1850s when Sacramento was the jumping off place for the diggings.*

Dominant landmark *in California's capital city is the golden-domed capitol building, completed in 1874. Forty acres of beautiful, well-manicured gardens surround it.*

465 Miles of Valley between the Coast and Sierra Ranges

JACK McDOWELL

TED STRESHINSKY

Rising behind acres *of alfalfa and a time-worn barn,*
fog-capped mountains hedge in the Central Valley's western
fringe. The long and narrow trough runs 465 miles long and
30 to 60 miles wide—with the Coast Range on the west,
the Sierra Nevada on the east.

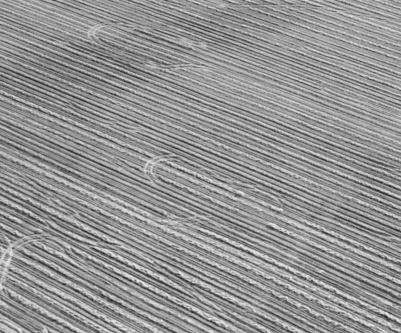

Neatly planted *(or recently plowed) plots of land growing various crops cover much of the Sacramento and San Joaquin valleys. Throughout the entire Central Valley, fertile fields surround isolated farmhouses, scattered farming communities, and a handful of cities.*

JACK McDOWELL

Heartland
of the Golden State

Rich soil, ample water *through irrigation, and a long growing season have made California's Central Valley one of the richest farm belts in the nation. More than 200 crops—from cotton, melons, and tomatoes in the San Joaquin Valley to rice (below) and almonds in the Sacramento Valley—yield some six billion dollars in harvests each year.*

JACK McDOWELL

Cotton

Melons

Tomatoes

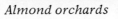

Almond orchards

Hub of California's Waterways

Artificial waterways *criss-cross the Central Valley, channeling river water from the wet northern half of the state to the dry southland. Controlling these massive water programs are the federal Central Valley Project and the California State Water Project (at left in the vicinity of Los Banos).*

LEE FOSTER

California's main river system *runs through the Central Valley, with the Sacramento River in the northern part and the San Joaquin in the southern part. They meet at the Delta (above), a maze of meandering waterways.*

TOM TRACY

The Northern
Mountains

One of California's most beautiful and least known regions stretches from the Coast Range east to the Nevada border, from the upper Sacramento Valley north to the Oregon border. This northern province is a wonderland of volcanic peaks and lava plateaus, serene lakes and rushing streams, jagged mountains and dense forests, small towns and hidden valleys.

Shasta is perhaps the area's most familiar name. Looming 14,161 feet, Mt. Shasta's snow-capped peak stands visible on a clear day for more than 100 miles. A sleeping giant in the volcanic Cascade Range, Shasta attracts skiers and snowshoers in winter, climbers in summer. To the south of Mt. Shasta lies Lake Shasta, a key reservoir in the Central Valley Project and a major boating recreation center.

Also in the Cascades, Lassen Volcanic National Park contains vestiges of the days when Lassen Peak blew its top. The Warner Mountains, an isolated spur of the Cascades, offer alpine and subalpine country reminiscent of the Sierra. In the Coast Range, pristine high country and low country stretch from Marble Mountain south to the Yolla Bolly-Middle Eel Wilderness.

Running through the middle of the Northern Mountains is Interstate 5. Several highways branch off this major thoroughfare and head west toward the Coast Range and east into the Cascades and over to the state's most remote corner.

Above timberline *at Marble Mountain Wilderness, bald ridges hold fossil marine organisms from an age when the mountains lay beneath shallow seas. Below timberline, the wilderness is a delightful world of glacial lakes, dense forests, and peaceful valleys.*

Marble Mountain South to Yolla Bolly... Untrampled Wilderness

Pristine forests *open onto colorful upland meadows in the Yolla Bolly-Middle Eel Wilderness, straddling the crest of the Coast Range. Logging roads to the wilderness boundary and narrow foot trails make accessible this gentle but remote area of quiet woodlands and rolling ridges.*

Natural Attractions around Shasta

Burney Creek's *beautiful twin falls plunge 129 feet into an emerald pool at McArthur-Burney Falls Memorial State Park. Behind the gushing waters, the swallowlike Black Swift makes its home in mossy crevices.*

Canada geese *whirr above foraging mule deer at Tule Lake National Wildlife Refuge in the Klamath Basin—a major stopover for millions of wildfowl moving south each fall along the Pacific Flyway.*

ROY MURPHY

DON NORMARK

Looming in icy grandeur *above fertile pasturelands, snow-capped Mt. Shasta (14,162 feet) dominates the landscape for 100 miles. The sleeping volcanic cone presents keen challenges to skiers and climbers.*

Smoke rose five miles *into the sky when "extinct" Lassen Peak erupted in 1915, spilling molten lava and floods of warm mud down its flanks and scalding bark off trees with horizontal blasts of steam. Northeast of the great plug dome —one in a long line along the Cascade Range—lies symmetrical Cinder Cone (right). This volcano was formed by an even fall of lava cinders.*

Lassen's Lunar Terrain

In Bumpass Hell, *one of the more desolate neighborhoods of Lassen Volcanic National Park, geothermal tumult shows itself in rising steam, hissing vents, and bubbling sulfur pools (left). The white in the pock-marked bank below is hard to recognize as a non-precious form of opal, which surfaces when lava decomposes without water. Parched clay (bottom of page) hems in a boiling mud pot.*

PHOTOS: DICK ROWAN

California's Remote Northeastern Corner

TOM TRACY

For generations—*until the arrival of the westward-bound white man—this sprawling territory of Modoc County belonged to Modoc, Pit, and Paiute Indians. For them, the rugged lava plateaus, fertile valleys, and towering Cascade mountains were "The Smiles of God."*

Still waters *stand shallow at glassy
Goose Lake, an alkaline expanse
that straddles the California-
Oregon border. Its waters reach
15-foot depths . . . at best.*

Descendants *of early homesteaders
still ranch in Surprise Valley at the
base of the steep eastern face
of the Warner Mountains. Emigrants
first entered the long, narrow graben
in 1849.*

Warner Mountains: Lush Valleys, Alpine Scenery, Solitude

Heavily timbered forests *on the western slopes of the Warner Mountains circle little ranch glens, like the one at Jess Valley. This mountainous highland—more compact and less rugged than the Sierra Nevada—lies within an isolated spur of the volcanic Cascade Range.*

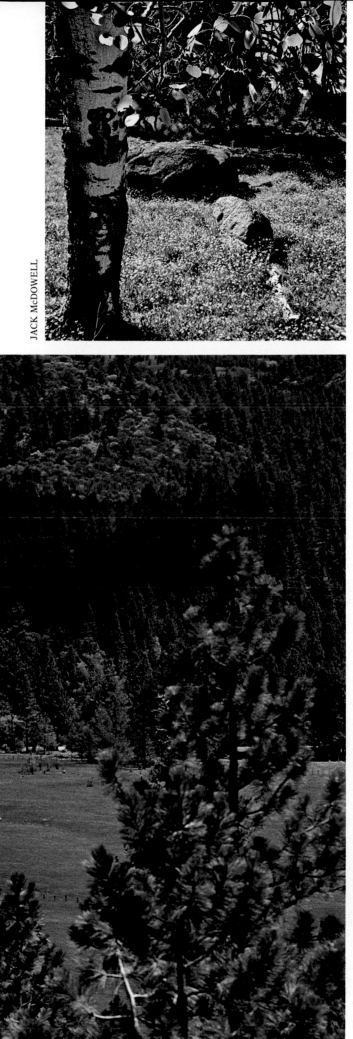

Definitely off the beaten path, *the South Warner Wilderness is a backpacker's delight. Summit Trail runs 27 miles along the crest of the Warner Mountains, whose ragged peaks sweep above alpine lakes and lush meadows. View from the trail takes in mountains and flatlands of three states— California, Oregon, and Nevada.*

THE NORTHERN MOUNTAINS **223**

Index

Aguanga, 147
Ahmanson Theater, 97
Alabama Hills, 164
Alcoa Building, 52
Allied Arts Guild, 66
Amador City, 193, 201
American River, 195, 200
Anacapa Island, 87
Anza-Borrego Desert State
  Park, 150-151
Arco Plaza, 94
Artist's Palette, 160-161
Audubon Canyon Ranch, 57
Avalon Bay, 112-113

Badwater, 158-159
Balboa Island, 127
Balboa Park, 136-137
Bank of America, 55
Banner, 146-147
Bay Area Rapid Transit, 64-65
Bayley's Folly, 192
Belvedere Island, 58-59
Berkeley, 54-55, 60-61
Big Sur, 80-81
Bishop, 165
Bodie, 166
Bristlecone pines, 166-167

Cable cars, 37, 46
Cabrillo National Monument,
  142-143
California State Water Project,
  210-211
Cannery, 42
Carmel, 76-77
Carmel Valley, 76-77
Carson house, 16
Cascades, 218-219, 220, 222-223
Central Coast, 70-89
Central Valley, 202-211
Central Valley Project, 210-211
Century City, 100-101
Channel Islands, 87
Chateau Chevalier, 27
Chinatown, 44-45
Christian Brothers, 26-27
Civic Center, Los Angeles, 96-97
Coachella Valley, 152
Coit Tower, 55
Coloma State Historic Park, 195
Columbia State Historic Park,
  194-195
Coronado Island, 140-141
Crescent City, 14-15
Crocker Gallery, 205

Death Valley National
  Monument, 156-161
Del Mar, 145
Delta, 211
Desert, 148-167
Devil's Golfcourse, 159
Devils Postpile, 184
Disneyland, 122-123
Dorothy Chandler Pavilion, 97
Drake's Beach, 20-21

East Bay, 55, 60-65
El Capitan, 172-173, 176
Embarcadero Plaza, 53
Emerald Bay, 170-171
Emigrant Wilderness, 180-181
Eureka, 16

Fairmont Hotel, 55
Farmer's Market, 101
Ferndale, 16
Ferry Building, 53
Fisherman's Wharf, Monterey, 73

Fisherman's Wharf, San
  Francisco, 42
Fort Point, 43

Gamble House, 116
Glorietta Bay, 140-141
Gold Rush Country, 190-201
Golden Gate Bridge, 36, 43, 55
Golden Gate National
  Recreation Area, 42-43
Golden Gate Park, 48-49
Golden Gateway, 40-41
Goose Lake, 221
Grace Cathedral, 51
Grauman's Chinese Theater, 103
Griffith Observatory, 105
Griffith Park, 104-105

Half Dome, 173, 177
Hanzell Winery, 26
Hearst Castle, 83
Heavenly Valley, 170
Hollywood, 102-103
Hollywood Bowl, 102-103
Hollywood Park, 98
Hotel del Coronado, 140-141
Humboldt Bay, 19
Huntington Beach, 127
Huntington Gardens, 117

J. Paul Getty Museum, 106-107
Jack London State Historic
  Park, 32
Jackson, 192-193, 198
Jess Valley, 222-223
John Muir Trail, 178-179
Joshua Tree National
  Monument, 154-155
Julian, 146-147
Justin Herman Plaza, 41

Kaweah Peaks, 186-187
Kennedy Mine, 192-193
Kings Canyon National Park,
  186-187
Klamath River, 19
Knott's Berry Farm, 125

La Jolla, 144
Lachryma Montis, 32
Lake Arrowhead, 121
Lake Merritt, 62-63
Lake Tahoe, 170-171
Lassen Volcanic National Park,
  218-219
Lawrence Hall of Science, 61
Lion Country Safari, 125
Lombard Street, 47
Los Angeles, 90-121
Los Angeles County Museum of
  Art, 101
Los Angeles Zoo, 105

MacArthur Park, 40
MacCallum House, 16
Malakoff Diggins State Historic
  Park, 196-197
Malibu, 106-107
Marble Mountain Wilderness,
  214-215
Marin County, 55, 56-59
Marin Headlands, 56
Marina del Rey, 109
Mariposa, 199
Maritime Plaza, 41, 52
Mark Taper Forum, 97
Marriott's Great America, 69
McArthur-Burney Falls
  Memorial State Park, 216
Mendocino, 16, 17
Menlo Park, 66, 67
Merced River, 174
Mills College, 61
Mission Bay, 134-135
Mission San Diego de Alcala, 131
Mission San Francisco Solano, 32
Mission Santa Barbara, 84

Modoc County, 220
Mokelumne Hill, 192
Mono Lake, 166
Monterey, 73
Monterey Peninsula, 72-75
Morro Bay, 82
Mt. Shasta, 216-217
Mt. Whitney, 179
Muir Woods National
  Monument, 57

Napa Valley, 22-31
Nevada City, 199, 200-201
Newport Bay, 126-127
Nob Hill, 46, 51
North Bay, 56-59
North Beach, 45
North Coast, 10-21
Northern Mountains, 212-223
Norton Simon Museum of Art,
  116-117
Noyo, 18

Oakland, 61, 62-63
Oakland Coliseum, 63
Oakland Museum, 62
Old Town San Diego State
  Historic Park, 130, 131
Olvera Street, 92-93
Ojai Valley, 89
Orange County, 122-127
Owens Valley, 164-165

Pacific Grove, 72-73
Palace of Fine Arts, 50
Palisade Glacier, 185
Palm Desert, 150-151
Palo Alto, 66-67
Palos Verdes Peninsula, 110-111
Pasadena, 114-117
Paul Masson's Mountain Winery,
  68
Pebble Beach, 74-75
Peninsula, 66-69
Pfeiffer Beach, 80
Pilot Hill, 192
Prairie Creek Redwoods State
  Park, 12
Presidio Hill, 130
Pt. Fermin State Park, 110
Pt. Lobos State Reserve, 78-79
Pt. Loma, 142-143
Pt. Reyes National Seashore,
  20-21

Rancho Los Cerritos, 93
Red Castle, 199
Redondo Beach, 109
Redwood National Park, 12-13
Redwoods, coast, 12-13, 15, 57
Redwoods, sequoia, 187
Richardson Bay, 58-59
Robert Mondavi Winery, 28
Rose Bowl, 114-115
Russian Hill, 47
Russian Holy Virgin Cathedral
  of the Church of Exile, 44

Sacramento, 204-205
Sacramento River, 211
Sacramento Valley, 206-209
San Bernardino Mountains,
  120-121
San Diego, 128-147
San Diego Zoo, 137, 138-139
San Francisco, 34-55, 65
San Francisco-Oakland Bay
  Bridge, 46, 55
San Gabriel Mountains, 118-119
San Jacinto Mountains, 153
San Joaquin River, 211
San Joaquin Valley, 206-209
San Jose, 69
San Juan Capistrano, 124
San Luis Obispo, 89
San Marino, 117

San Pedro, 110
San Simeon, 83
Santa Barbara, 84-87
Santa Catalina Island, 112-113
Santa Clara, 69
Santa Cruz, 68
Santa Lucia Mountains, 80-81, 83
Santa Monica Bay, 108-109
Santa Monica Boulevard,
  100-101
Santa Ynez Mountains, 86-87
Santa Ynez Valley, 88
Santa Ysabel, 147
Saratoga, 68
Sausalito, 58-59
Sea World, 135
Sequoia National Park, 186-187
Sequoias, 187
Serra Museum, 130
Seventeen-mile Drive, 74-75
Shelter Island, 132-133
Sierra Nevada, 168-189
Solvang, 88
Sonoma Mission, 32
Sonoma Valley, 22-33
Sonoma Vineyards, 28-29
Sonora, 199
South Warner Wilderness, 223
Souverain of Alexander Valley,
  27
St. Francis Hotel, 39
St. Mary's Cathedral, 53
St. Sava's Serbian Orthodox
  Church, 198
Stanford University, 66-67
Stanislaus River, 200
Sterling Winery, 26, 29
Sunset Magazine and Sunset
  Books, 67
Surprise Valley, 211
Sutter Creek, 201

Telegraph Hill, 47
Telescope Peak, 158-159
Tiburon, 58-59
Torrey Pines State Reserve, 145
Transamerica Pyramid, 52-53,
  55
Tule Lake National Wildlife
  Refuge, 216
Tuolumne Meadows, 178
Twin Peaks, 54-55

Ubehebe Crater, 159
Union Square, 38, 39
Universal Studios, 102
University of California at
  Berkeley, 60-61
University of California at
  Los Angeles, 101
University of Southern
  California, 99

Vaillancourt Fountain, 41, 53
Vallejo Home, 32
Ventana Wilderness, 80
Vernal Falls, 174-175

Walnut Creek, 65
Warner Mountains, 221, 222-223
Watts Towers, 98-99
Wayfarer's Chapel, 110
Wilshire Boulevard, 100-101
Winchester Mystery House, 69
Wine Country, 22-33
Wolf House, 32
Woodward fountain, 41

Yolla Bolly-Middle Eel
  Wilderness, 215
Yosemite Falls, 176
Yosemite National Park,
  172-177, 178

Zabriskie Point, 161
Zuma Beach, 106